Tin Whistle Tutor

Eithne and John Vallely

Tin Whistle Tutor

First published in 2008 by
Appletree Press Ltd
The Old Potato Station
14 Howard Street South
Belfast BT7 1AP

Tel: +44 (028) 90 24 30 74
Fax: +44 (028) 90 24 67 56
Email: reception@appletree.ie
Web: www.appletree.ie

A catalogue record for this book is available from the British Library.

First published in 1976 as *Making Music – The Tin Whistle* by Appletree Press Ltd

Tin Whistle Tutor

ISBN-13: 978 1 84758 004 7

Desk and Marketing Editor: Jean Brown
Copy-editing: Jim Black
Designer: Stuart Wilkinson
Production Manager: Paul McAvoy

9 8 7 6 5 4 3 2 1

AP3412

Contents

Contents

Introduction

1. The book and the music has been divided into seven sections, containing musical theory and a selection of tunes. Try to master each section before moving on to the next. You can follow the tunes from the written music and then play along with the music on the website. Always refer to the website when you see the following symbol.

 www.irelandseye.com/music/tinwhistle

2. At the beginning of the book completed diagrams above each note illustrate the fingering to be used on the tin whistle. Later on the diagrams are not completed, and you may like to fill these in yourself.

Notes and Notation

There are two factors which
music notation must indicate
– pitch and rhythm

Pitch

The relative highness or lowness of a note is known as *The Pitch*.

Music is usually written on 5 lines called *The Stave* and these lines indicate the pitch of each note.

The following symbol will be seen on the Stave at the beginning of each tune to be played on the tin whistle.

This symbol is derived from the letter G and gives its name to the *treble* or *'G' Clef*. The notes are written on the 5 lines and in the spaces between them. *

The notes on the Treble Clef are as follows. *

An easy way to memorise the notes on the Treble Clef is to use mnemonics. The sentence *Every Good Boy Deserves Fruit* will remind you of the notes on the lines E G B D F. The notes in the four spaces spell F A C E

Extra notes can be placed above and below the Stave. These give us D and High G.

Notes below D and above High G are written on short extra lines called Leger Lines.

Rhythm

In music there are different kinds of notes to indicate the
length or duration of each note.

♩ or ♩ is a MINIM and gets 2 beats.

♩ or ♩ is a CROTCHET and gets 1 beat.

♪ or ♪ is a QUAVER and gets 1/2 beat.

♪ or ♪ is a SEMI-QUAVER and gets 1/4 beat.

When two quavers are played together they are

usually joined like this ♫ or ♫

Semi-quavers are joined in the same way

A dot placed immediately after a note lengthens it by half.

♩. = 3 beats.   ♪. = 3/4 beat.

♩. = 1 1/2 beats.

Playing the Notes

The Whistle

The tin whistle which we use in this course is in the key of D and this is the one which we recommend.

If you look at your whistle you will notice that it consists of a cylindrical metal tube with six finger holes and a plastic mouthpiece.

How to Hold...
The tin whistle is held as in the diagram with both thumbs on the back to support it. The little fingers which are not used for playing can also help to balance the whistle.

How to Blow...
Place the mouthpiece between the lips and blow gently, without covering any of the finger-holes. Concentrate on getting an even steady note. If you are getting a high-pitched, shrill sound, you are blowing too hard. Listen to the correct sound on the website, and try and copy what you hear.

How to Play...
The notes are obtained by covering and uncovering the 6 holes on the front of the whistle and blowing gently.

Left Hand Notes
(LH = left hand, RH = right hand)

To play B

Put the 1st finger of your LH on the top finger hole nearest the mouthpiece, keeping the left thumb on the back for support. Make sure that the hole is completely covered by your finger.

To play A

Keep the top hole covered, cover the 2nd hole with the 2nd finger of the LH. This will give you A.

To play G

Keeping the top 2 holes covered, place the 3rd finger of the LH on the 3rd hole from the top. This will give you G.

Practice these 3 notes until they sound as they do on the website. If you still produce squeaky notes, you are probably not covering the holes completely. When you are satisfied that you are getting the LH notes correctly, you can go on to the RH notes.

Right Hand Notes

To play F#

Keeping the top 3 notes covered, place the 1st finger of the RH on the 4th hole, using the right thumb to balance it at the back. This will give you the note F#. (To sharpen a note is to raise it by a semi-tone)

To play E

E is produced by covering the 5th hole with the 2nd finger of the RH keeping all the notes above it covered as before.

To play D

Now cover the 6th hole with the 3rd finger of the RH keeping all the holes above it covered also. This will give you D.

Practice all these notes in conjunction with the website, paying special attention to the lower notes.

To play C

C or natural C is played by covering the 2nd and 3rd holes with 2nd and 3rd fingers of LH.
(C natural occurs in tunes in the key of G: – those which have one sharp (#) at the beginning.)

To play C#

C sharp is played with all the finger holes uncovered. (This note occurs in tunes in the key of D: – those with 2 sharps at the beginning.)

To play High D

High D is obtained by covering all holes except the top one with the correct fingers.

These notes, D to High D, are the 1st octave. Notes on the 2nd octave are shown in Section 3.

Breath Control
This is an important factor in playing any wind instrument. If you take too many breaths you will produce a very choppy sound. Take a deep breath at the beginning of the tune which will carry you through to the end of the phrase.
(Phrases are marked thus $\checkmark$)

Playing the Tunes

How to Get Started

The notes required for each tune are shown at the start of each piece. Check that you can play them before attempting the tunes. Listen to each tune on the website a few times, following it in the music. To help you diagrams of each note have been drawn until the end of section 5. Fill in uncompleted diagrams to help you learn the notes.

Deus Meus Adiuva Me

11th Century Hymn (My God Come to My Aid)
E.D.F#.G.B.A.C.

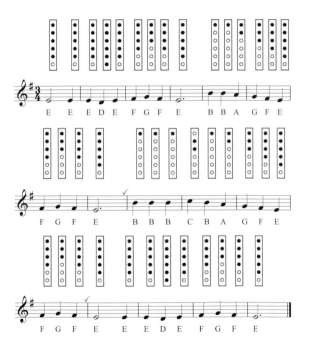

Hymn to Saint Patrick

D.E.F#.G.A.B.C.D'

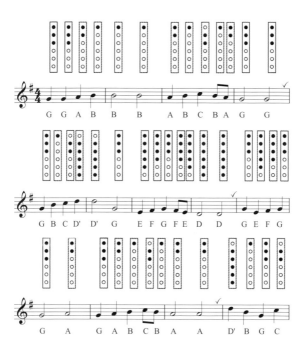

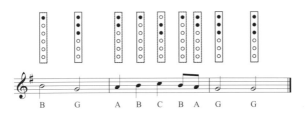

B   G   A   B   C   B   A   G   G

Croagh Patrick, Co. Mayo

Eileen Aroon

D.E.F#.G.A.B.C.D'

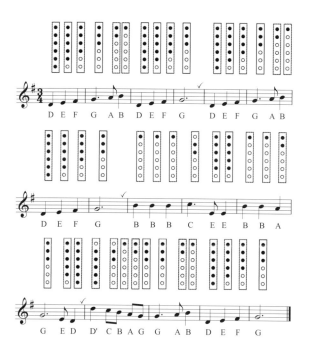

D E F G A B D E F G   D E F G A B

D E F G   B B C E E B B A

G E D D' C B A G G A B D E F G

My Aunt Jane

D.E.G.A.B.C.D'

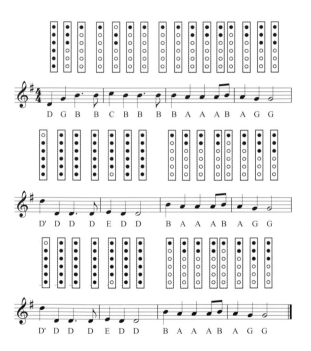

Second Octave and Time Signatures

Second Octave

The second octave is obtained by using the same fingering as the first octave but blowing harder. Listen to the website again and play the notes from High E to Top D.

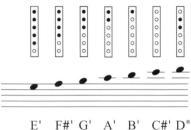

E'   F#' G'   A'   B'   C#' D"

Bar Lines

If you listen carefully to the tunes on the website you will notice that some notes get a heavier beat (sound louder) than others, and that these heavy beats occur regularly every 2, 3 or 4 beats. Now look at the music and you will see that there is a vertical line in front of each accented note. This is called a *Bar line* and the music between each bar line is called a *Bar*.

At the end of a tune or at the end of a section of a tune there is a *double Bar line*.

Where the double bar line is preceded by two dots you should repeat that section of the tune once from the previous double bar line. If there is no double bar line earlier in the tune, repeat once from the beginning.

Time Signatures

At the beginning of each tune you will see the *Time Signature*, which consists of two numbers, one above the other. The top figure tells us the number of beats in the bar, and the bottom one the type of beat.

The most common Time Signatures are as follows:–

This means three crotchets or their equivalent in each bar.

This means 4 crotchets or their equivalent (i.e. eight quavers) in a bar, and is the most common time signature, occurring in marches, reels, polkas, hornpipes, etc. It is also known as Common Time and indicated thus.

2 crotchets or their equivalent in each bar and is sometimes used instead or 4 4 in reels, hornpipes and polkas.

6 quavers or their equivalent in each bar. It is found mostly in jigs and some marches and set dances.

9 quavers or their equivalent to each bar and in Irish Music this denotes a Slip Jig.

Two notes joined by this symbol above are played as one note. Here the note A is held for two beats.

Triplets

Three notes linked together as shown above are played in one beat. In the next set of tunes we have two marches and a simple polka in 4 4 time, and a ballad tune in 3 4 time.

The Dawning of the Day

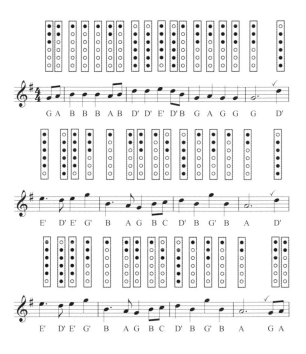

G A   B   B   B   A B   D' D' E' D'B   G   A G   G   G   D'

E'   D' E' G'   B   A G   B C   D' B   G' B   A   D'

E'   D' E' G'   B   A G   B C   D' B   G' B   A   G A

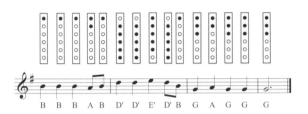

B B B A B D' D' E' D' B G A G G G

Sunrise over Dublin

The Mountains of Pomeroy

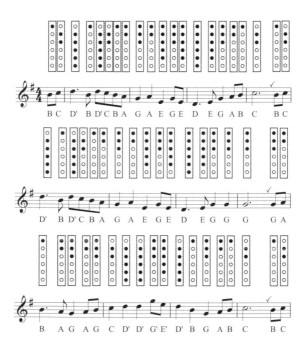

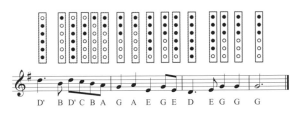

D' BD'CBA GA E GE D EGG G

Beaghmore Stone Circle, Co. Tyrone

Polka

D.E.G.A.B.C.D'

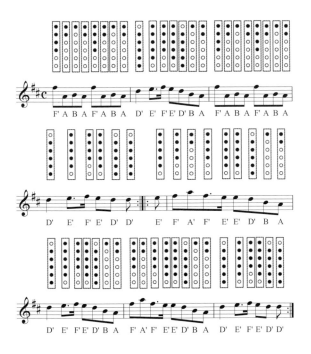

Spancil Hill

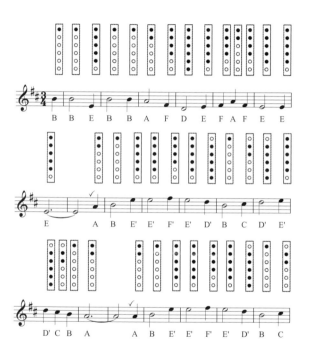

B B E B B A F D E F A F E E

E A B E' E' F' E' D' B C D' E'

D' C B A A B E' E' F' E' D' B C

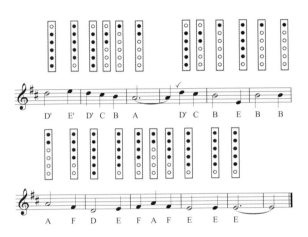

Section 4

Ornamentation

What is Ornamentation?

Ornamentation is one of the main characteristics of Irish traditional music and what makes it so distinctive. This section contains four slow airs all of which have some ornamentation.

As these are in fact song airs, the time is not observed as strictly as in dance music because it is the words which decide the rhythm of the song. Therefore you must learn these tunes in conjunction with the website.

Grace Notes

Some of the airs are ornamented by adding extra notes or grace notes. These are written in very small type and should be played quickly as an embellishment.

Sliding

A slide from one note to the next above it occurs sometimes in these airs. This is done by easing the finger slowly off the finger-hole instead of lifting it straight off. It is indicated in the music by a curved arrow.

Vibrato

Long notes are sometimes ornamented by the use of Vibrato. This is a 'shake' and is porducted by moving the 2nd finger below the note being played quickly up and down off the whistle. If we wish to play vibrato on F# the 3rd finger of the RH is shaken over the 6th finger hole. We have indicated it by the symbol V.

The Mermaid

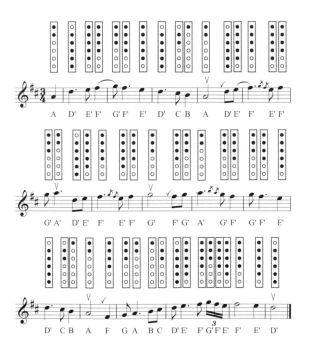

Goodbye to Moy

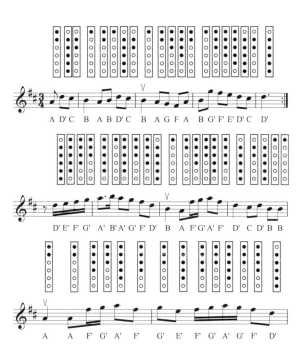

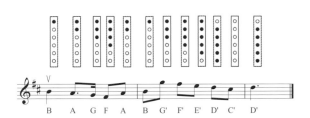

B   A   G   F   A   B   G'   F'   E'   D'   C'   D'

The Moy River, Sligo

The Fairy Child

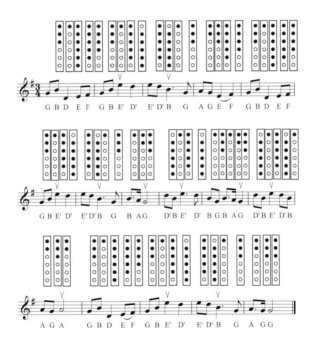

Faithful Brown Cow

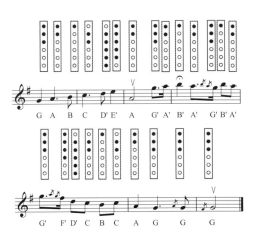

G   A   B   C   D' E'   A   G' A' B' A'   G' B' A'

G' F' D' C B C   A   G   G   G

Dance Rhythms

Dance Rhythms

The tunes in this section include two different dance rhythms which all require a type of ornamentation called rolling.

The tunes themselves feature two of the main Irish dance rhythms – hornpipe and reel.

Rolling
This is the most characteristic form of ornamentation used in Irish Music and is basically the playing of grace notes above and below the note to be ornamented.

An A roll would be written as shown above.

Listen to these rolls as played on the website and practise them thoroughly before trying any of the tunes.

Cranning

This form of ornamentation is used on the low E and D notes and is the characteristic ornamentation employed in piping. The E cran is played as follows:

The D cran is played as shown below:

These are difficult forms of ornamentation and need *much* practice beforew they can be incorporated into tunes.

Cronin's Hornpipe

B A G A B D' D' B D' E' G' A' G' E' D' E' G' A'

B' A' G' E' D' B G A B A A G A C B A

G A B D' D' B D' E' G' A' G' E' D' E' G' A'

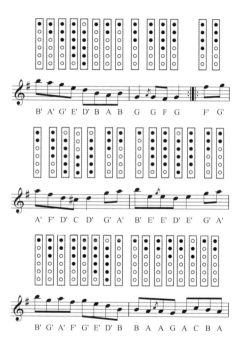

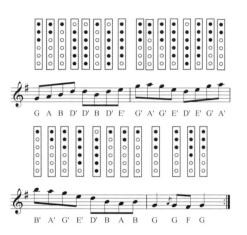

G A B D' D' B D' E' G' A' G' E' D' E' G' A'

B' A' G' E' D' B A B G G F G

Over the Door to Maggie

This tune is more difficult than the rest, but it illustrates the kind of traditional playing which is probably most associated with the tin whistle. The main feature of the ornamentation to note is the continuous rolling, particularly on A and G, both in the low octave and in the high octave

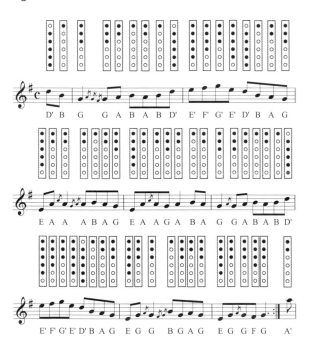

D' B G   G A B A B D' E' F' G' E' D' B A G

E A A   A B A G   E A A G A B A G   G A B A B D'

E' F' G' E' D' B A G   E G G   B G A G   E G G F G   A'

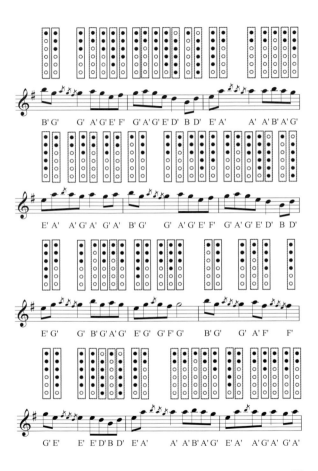

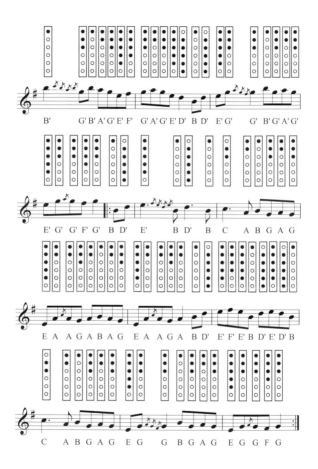

B' G'B'A'G'E'F' G'A'G'E'D' B D' E'G' G' B'G'A'G'

E'G' G'F'G' B D' E' B D' B C A B G A G

EA AGABAG EA AGA B D' E'F'E'B D'E'D'B

C ABGAG EG G BGAG EGGFG

Other Tunes to Try

Father O'Flynn

A D'A F D F A D'E'D'C B A D'C D'E'F'G' F E'F'E'C A

D'A F D F A D'E'D'C B A D'C D'E'F'G' F'D'D'D'   G'

F'D'F'F'G'A' E'F'E'E'C A D'C D'B E'D' C A A A C

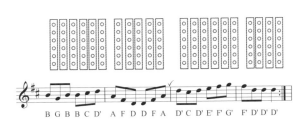

B G B B C D' A F D D F A D' C D' E' F' G' F' D' D' D'

Tatter Jack Welch

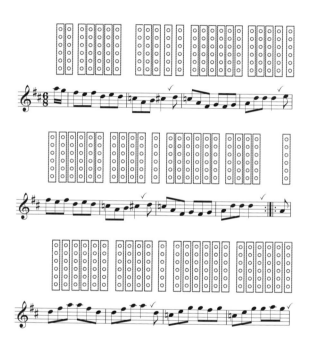

The Morning Star

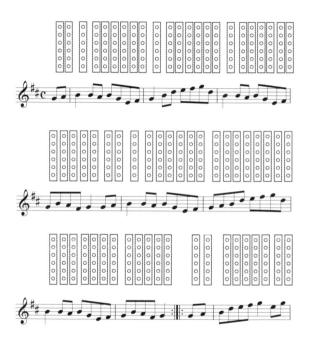

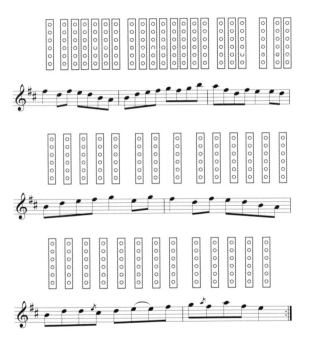

The Plains of Boyle

Father Dollard's Favourite

Planxty Irwin

In the two bars where two sets of notes are given, I have included the top line as an alternative to the lower C#. This is often preferred by pipers, but is too low for the 'D' whistle.

The Dear Irish Boy

The First House in Connacht

Irish Cottage

Write Your Own

Write Your Own

This section allows you to have a go at writing your own tunes. Alternatively copy down tunes that you like from friends and watch your musical repertoire grow.

Acknowledgements

page 4 © istockphoto.com/Timothy Large
page 8 © istockphoto.com/Eric Etman
page 12 © istockphoto.com/Judy Picciotto
page 14 © istockphoto.com/Bertrand Collet
page 7,16,18,20,24,32,58,59 © istockphoto.com/Diego Vargas
page 22 © istockphoto.com/Jason Wagner
page 27 © istockphoto.com/Jane McIlroy
page 30 © istockphoto.com/Andrija Kova
page 37 © istockphoto.com/eferkr
page 39 © Northern Ireland Tourist Board
page 40 © istockphoto.com/Ryan K.C. Wong
page 44 © istockphoto.com/Donall O'Cleirigh
page 48 © istockphoto.com/Andreas Kasper
page 51 © istockphoto.com/Brian Tansey
page 52 © istockphoto.com/Thomas Gordon
page 55 © istockphoto.com/ Mike Dabell
page 56 © istockphoto.com/Gary Nash
page 60 © istockphoto.com/José Luis Gutiérrez
page 63 © istockphoto.com/Ula Kapala
page 67 © istockphoto.com/Donall O'Cleirigh
page 68 © istockphoto.com/Judy Picciotto
page 71 © istockphoto.com/Kelvin Wakefield
page 73 © istockphoto.com/Kurt Gordon
page 76 © istockphoto.com/Stephen Bonk
page 83 © istockphoto.com/Joan Champ
page 84 © istockphoto.com/Laura Callaghan

Index to Tunes